Flavours of Prince Edward Island

Classic Recipes and Historic Photographs

J.J. Sharp

NIMBUS PUBLISHING LIMITED

Nimbus Publishing Limited
P.O. Box 9301, Stn. A
Halifax, Nova Scotia
B3K 5N5

Design: Kathy Kaulbach, Halifax
Cover photograph: A parlour mantle, 1895 (Public Archives of Prince Edward Island)
Title-page photograph: Tea at Government House with Dr. A.C. MacDonald, c. 1918 (Public Archives of Prince Edward Island)
Back-cover photograph: Jack Martin
Photographs: Public Archives of Prince Edward Island (the P.E.I. Heritage Foundation Collection and the Charlottetown Camera Club Collection) and I.L. Rogers, *Charlottetown—Its Life in Its Buildings*

Recipe sources: *The York Cook Book,* York United Church Women; *Sharing Our Favourites,* Women's Institute of Prince Edward Island; and *The Anniversary Cook Book,* Anglican Church Women, Cathedral Church of St. Peter

Canadian Cataloguing in Publication Data

Sharp, J.J. (James Jack), 1939-
Flavours of Prince Edward Island
ISBN 0-921054-45-9
1. Cookery, Canadian—Prince Edward Island style.
I. Title.

TX715.6.S52 1990   641.59717   C90-097534-2

Printed and bound in Canada

CONTENTS

INTRODUCTION

First called Abegweit, "cradled by the waves," by the Indians who inhabited the island before the white man came, the fertile island in the Gulf of St. Lawrence has had a chequered history and a variety of names. Discovered by Jacques Cartier in 1534, the land already had the character of a garden. Cartier described it as of great quality, the land being "low and plaine and the fairest that may possibly be seene, full of goodly medowes and trees." By 1603, the land was known to be an island and had been given the name Ile Saint-Jean.

Initially, the French planned to turn the island into a breadbasket for the main French fortress at Louisbourg, Cape Breton, but organizing the settlements proved difficult. As late as 1735, fewer than 450 people inhabited Ile Saint-Jean. Plagues of mice devastated the crops on a number of occasions, and these were so bad that a town was named Souris after the French word for "mouse." In time, things improved and immigration increased so that, by 1750, more than 2,000 people called the island home. But a few years later, they fell to the British and most were evicted forcibly. Today, little remains of the original French presence.

After the English wrested control in 1758, they simply translated the French name for the island to "Island of St. John," but that led to confusion with similarly named towns in Newfoundland and New Brunswick. In 1799 the island was given the name it holds today. Repression at home forced many Scots to emigrate and, though most ended up in neighbouring Nova Scotia, a goodly number chose to try the new Island of Prince Edward. Most of these settlers had a hard time getting themselves established, but eventually they settled down to a routine similar to that which they had known at home. Many of their staple foods could be had in the new land: Porridge was made easily from the oats they grew, and potatoes grew easily in the rich soil. These, together with the herring that swarmed around the coasts, provided a diet full of nourishment. Even today, Scots sing of "tatties and herring."

When the American colonies separated from the motherland, nearly 50,000 loyalists came north to Canada. Many found the mild climate of Prince Edward Island to their liking and settled there. By 1780 almost one-fifth of the island's population had come from that source. But more Scots were yet to arrive. A few years after the United Empire Loyalist immigration, there was an influx of the group of Scots known as the Skye Pioneers or Selkirk Settlers. Population growth was rapid in the early nineteenth century, with a flood of immigrants from all parts of Britain and Ireland. These people merged with the earlier settlers and eventually took their part in the formation of Canada, holding the first meeting to discuss national confederation in Charlottetown in 1864.

Prince Edward Island is well known as the garden of Atlantic Canada. With its rich, red soil and mild climate, it is one of the most productive areas in the region, famous, among other things, for its potatoes. From its earliest days it has been a farming land. Writing in 1820, a Scot named Walter Johnstone described how most people lived on a diet of "wheaten bread, potatoes, codfish, herrings and pork, with tea of some kind or other or milk." He went on to mention the "great numbers of lobsters, oysters and various other kinds of shell-fish … with great banks of mussels in several of the rivers." Even then, the islanders were exporting their goods, "grain and potatoes to Newfoundland; and grain, pork and potatoes to Miramichi, and grain and potatoes to Halifax." Times have changed, but it can still be said that "the Islanders enjoy a privilege … in cultivating the ground (which is) so very grateful that no man ever yet bestowed prudent labour upon it but it repaid him for his toil."

POTATO FLOUNDER SOUP

2 onions
2 Tbsp butter
2 Tbsp flour
1 lb potatoes, peeled and chopped
2 medium carrots, peeled and chopped
1 tomato, skinned and chopped
1 cup white wine
6 cups water
Salt and pepper
1 lb flounder fillets
Large pinch thyme
1/2 cup thick cream

Finely chop onions and sauté gently in butter. When onion is soft but not browned, add flour and stir well. Add vegetables and stir to coat with flour. Add wine, water, salt, and pepper and cook until vegetables are tender, about 20 minutes. Add thyme and fish broken into pieces and simmer 10 minutes. Before serving, fold in cream.

HAM-BONE SOUP

3/4 cup split peas
1 large potato, chopped
3/4 cup sliced carrots
1/2 cup diced turnip
1 onion
1 Tbsp drippings
2 pts water
1 ham bone
Salt and pepper

Wash peas and drain. Put in pan with vegetables and drippings, cover and simmer gently 20 minutes, stirring occasionally. Add water and bone. Season. Bring to a boil and cook gently 2 to 2 1/2 hours or until peas are tender. Remove ham bone and serve.

Ice cutting on the lake

EGGPLANT AND CRAB

2 medium eggplants
Salt
5 Tbsp corn oil
Pepper
Pinch cayenne pepper
2 tsp paprika
Pinch oregano
2 medium onions
2 tomatoes, chopped
1 Tbsp tomato paste
1 cup crab meat
2 Tbsp Parmesan cheese
2 Tbsp melted butter

Clean eggplants, remove stems, and cut in half lengthwise. Sprinkle salt onto cut surface and leave half an hour. Wash to remove excess salt and fry in oil with cut side down until it turns brown. Bake in 350°F oven 10 minutes or until tender. Meanwhile, add spices to oil in which eggplant was fried and fry a few minutes to bring out flavour. Chop onion and add, cooking until soft but not brown. Add tomatoes and tomato paste and simmer gently until thickened. Scoop flesh from eggplants and add flesh to mixture. Cook a few minutes and add crab meat. When all is hot, return mixture to eggplant shells. Sprinkle with cheese and melted butter and grill until cheese is nicely browned.

The most common island crab is the rock crab, which grows to about four or five inches on average. They are found in bays and inlets, often around piers and other man-made structures. They are easy to catch and quite delicious.

Market Square, 1873-1883

CLAM CHOWDER

1/2 cup diced salt pork fat
2 medium onions
1 medium potato
2 cups clam juice
2 cups fresh, cooked clams
2 cups milk
Salt and pepper
Chopped parsley

Fry salt pork in a deep pan until brown and crisp. Remove scraps and save for later. Chop onion and fry gently in melted fat. Peel and dice potato and add with clam juice to pan. Cover and simmer about 15 minutes until potato is soft. Clean clams carefully and add milk, clams, salt, and pepper to mixture. Heat gently until just about to boil and serve, sprinkling pork scraps and parsley on top of each serving.

Note: Sand can be removed from clams by standing them a few hours in fresh salt water to which a cup of oatmeal has been added.

The Indians gave the name "quahog" to the hard-shelled clams that live at and just below the low-water mark. They do not bury themselves deep and can be dug up easily. The larger ones, up to five inches long, tend to be tough and are best used chopped up in chowders. The smaller ones are often referred to as cherry-stone clams.

Picnic party, 1894

FISH CHOWDER

1 lb fish fillets
1/4 cup chopped onion
1 cup chopped carrot
1/4 cup chopped celery
2 Tbsp butter
1/4 cup flour
1/2 tsp salt
1/4 tsp pepper
1/4 tsp paprika
2 cups chicken stock
3 cups milk

Cut fish into small cubes. Sauté onion, carrot, and celery in butter until onion is tender but not browned. Blend in flour and spices. Gradually add stock and milk, stirring continuously until mixture has thickened. Add fish and simmer until it is cooked, about 10 to 15 minutes.

CORN CHOWDER

6 slices bacon
1 onion, chopped
3 cups warm water
2 cups fresh corn kernels
OR 1 large can cream corn
1 1/2 cups chopped, raw potato
3 Tbsp butter
1 cup evaporated milk
Salt and pepper
Pinch paprika

Sauté bacon and onion until bacon is almost crisp and onion is cooked but not browned. Add water, corn, and potato and simmer until potato is tender. Add butter, milk, salt, and pepper. Return to a boil. If necessary, thicken with cornstarch. Serve sprinkled with a little paprika.

Engineers at work, 1898

OYSTER PIE

2 medium potatoes
Pastry for pie
2 cups shucked oysters, with juice
4 hard-boiled eggs
2 Tbsp butter
Salt and pepper

Boil potatoes until almost cooked. Slice thinly, put pie crust bottom in dish, and arrange potatoes on top. Drain oysters and lay on top of potatoes. Slice eggs, arrange on top, and dot with butter. Add oyster juice and season to taste. Cover with pastry and slit to allow steam to escape. Bake 10 minutes in 400°F oven. Lower heat to 375°F and cook 20 minutes or until pie crust is nicely browned.

ANGELS ON HORSEBACK

24 raw, shucked oysters
2 Tbsp lemon juice
Pinch salt
1/2 tsp Tabasco sauce
1 tsp Worcestershire sauce
12 slices bacon

Drain oysters and dry on paper towel. Place in bowl and add lemon juice, salt, and both sauces. Stir gently until oysters are coated in mixture. Cut bacon slices in half and wrap each oyster in half a slice, securing it with a small toothpick. Place in baking dish and cook at 450°F until bacon is crisp. Serve immediately.

Prince Edward Island is well known for its oysters, which were once so cheap they were known as food for the poor. Found in estuaries and bays, their shape varies depending on the bed on which they grow. Flat, rocky, uncrowded beds provide the best oysters—shells four to six inches round and deeply cupped.

Behind Province House, Charlottetown, c. 1895

POTTED CHRISTMAS HOCK

2 lb stewing beef
3 pork hocks
1/2 tsp mixed spice
1/2 tsp cloves
Salt and pepper
1/2 tsp cinnamon
1/2 tsp mace

Wash meat and simmer 3 hours in large pot. Remove meat and drain, then put through a mincer or grinder and set aside. Boil hocks for as long as necessary to remove gelatin. Remove hocks and strain. Put spices in a muslin bag and tie tightly. Add spice bag to liquid and continue to boil until volume is halved. Remove spice bag and return ground meat to pot, mixing well. Put mixture into bowls wetted with cold water and set aside until firm.

Note: This is an old recipe often cooked for a light Christmas snack. Nowadays it's possible to use pickling spice and to purchase the gelatin instead of boiling hocks.

Vinnicomb's Band, c. 1900

SOLOMON GUNDY

6 salt herring
2 Tbsp pickling spice
4 cups white vinegar
1 1/2 cups sugar
2 onions

Soak herring overnight, skin, and cut into 2-inch pieces. Put pickling spice in a muslin bag and bring vinegar, sugar, and spice to a boil. Peel and slice onions. Arrange alternate layers of fish and onion in sterilized jars. Allow vinegar to cool, remove spice, and pour over fish. Seal jars tightly and leave at least 3 weeks.

Courthouse, with city officials, c. 1870

PEPPER STEAK

2 lb sirloin tip steak
2 cloves garlic
1/2 cup soya sauce
1 cup onion
1 cup green pepper
1 cup celery

Cut steak into thin strips. Rub with garlic and marinate in half the soya sauce, preferably overnight but at least 2 hours. Sauté gently in frying pan, add onions and rest of soya sauce. Cook 20 minutes and add green pepper and celery. Cook 10 more minutes and serve.

CHERRY-GLAZED BAKED HAM

6-lb uncooked ham
1 large can cherry pie filling
1 cup orange marmalade
1/4 cup sherry
1/4 cup orange juice

Bake ham until almost done and remove from heat. Pour drippings and fat from pan. Score surface of ham lightly in a diamond pattern and return to pan. Remove cherries from filling and save them, mixing filling with marmalade, sherry, and orange juice. Pour over ham and return to oven. Continue baking until ham is ready, basting often. Serve garnished with reserved cherries.

Meat market, Market Building, Queen's Square, Charlottetown

LAMB STEW WITH DUMPLINGS

Stew:
1 1/2 lb boneless stewing lamb
2 Tbsp butter
2 onions
1 clove garlic
Flour
1/2 tsp thyme
2 tsp salt
Pinch pepper
2 2/3 cups water
6 medium carrots
1 1/2 lb Brussels sprouts
Dumplings:
1 1/2 cups flour
1 Tbsp baking powder
1 tsp salt
1 Tbsp dried mint leaves
1/4 cup margarine
Milk

Trim any excess fat from lamb and cut into bite-sized pieces. Brown meat in butter and remove from pan. Chop onion, crush garlic, and sauté until onion is tender. Return meat to pan and sprinkle with flour. Cook a few minutes and add seasoning and water. Cover and simmer 1 hour. Slice carrots and add with Brussels sprouts to stew. Top with dumplings. Cover and cook another 20 minutes.

To make dumplings, combine dry ingredients and cut in margarine. Stir in enough milk to form a soft dough. Form into dumplings and cook as above.

Bringing in supplies, Prowse Bros., Charlottetown, c. 1900

LAMB SHOULDER HOTPOT

4 medium potatoes
2 Tbsp oil
1/4 cup chopped green pepper
2 small onions
1 Tbsp chopped celery
4 sliced mushrooms
1/2 cup fresh peas
1/2 cup carrots
4 lamb shoulder chops
2 cups stock
Salt and pepper

Dice potatoes and prepare vegetables. Sauté potatoes in oil with green pepper and onions 3 minutes. Remove from pan and sauté celery and mushrooms 3 minutes. Arrange potatoes around base of fireproof dish. Add other vegetables, top with chops, and pour on stock. Cover and cook 1 hour, 15 minutes in 350°F oven. Season to taste.

HONEY-GLAZED LEG OF LAMB

4- to 6-lb leg of lamb
1 tsp basil
1 tsp salt
1/2 tsp pepper
1/4 cup honey
1/4 cup mustard
2 Tbsp soft butter

Rub leg with basil, salt, and pepper. Place in roasting pan and cook in 325°F oven, about 20 minutes per pound. Make glaze by mixing honey, mustard, and butter. Spread onto leg about 20 minutes before it is done and raise temperature to 400°F. Baste occasionally until leg is ready.

Murray Harbour Railway Station

DUCK IN RED-WINE SAUCE

1-lb roast duck, without bone
1 small onion
1 Tbsp fresh parsley
1/2 orange
Fresh thyme
1 bay leaf
Chicken bouillon cube
1 oz butter
1/2 oz flour
1 cup hot water
1/2 cup red wine
Salt and pepper

Cut duck into slices. Chop onion and parsley. Grate orange and wash fresh herbs carefully. Dissolve bouillon cube in a little hot water. Melt butter in pan and add flour, stirring to avoid lumps. Gradually add hot water and wine, stirring as mixture thickens. Continue stirring until it boils. Simmer everything approximately 45 minutes. Season to taste and remove bay leaf before serving.

HONEY-GINGER CHICKEN

2 Tbsp chopped onion
2 tsp soya sauce
1/4 cup honey
2 Tbsp lemon juice
1/4 cup vegetable oil
2 tsp garlic salt
1 tsp salt
2 tsp ginger
1/2 cup orange juice
2 1/2 lb chicken breasts

Mix all ingredients other than chicken to make a sauce. Arrange chicken in oven-proof dish and pour on sauce. Cover and bake 40 minutes in 375°F oven. Uncover and cook 10 more minutes, basting occasionally.

Duck-shooting on the marshes

BAKED HADDOCK

1 lb haddock fillets
2 onions
1 tomato
Butter
Milk
Salt and pepper
Cheddar cheese

Place fillets in baking dish. Slice onions and tomatoes and lay on top. Dot liberally with butter and add enough milk to almost cover fillets. Add salt and pepper to taste. Cover and bake in 325°F oven about 1 hour. Remove from oven, cover with grated cheese, and grill until cheese has melted.

Note: This can be prepared easily and quickly on a barbecue. Put fillets in a foil pouch and proceed as above, but omit milk.

CREAMED COD

1 lb salt cod
3 Tbsp butter
3 Tbsp flour
1 1/2 cups milk
Dash pepper
Dash mace
Sprig fresh parsley

Soak fish overnight in cold water. Discard water and soak again in fresh, cold water 2 to 3 hours to remove salt. Drain well and wash. Poach gently about 15 minutes in fresh water and serve with sauce.

To make sauce, melt butter and add flour. While stirring continuously, add milk. When thickened, add pepper, mace, and chopped parsley.

Tennis players, Victoria Park, Charlottetown, 1889

CAMPFIRE TROUT IN CORN HUSKS

1 whole, fresh trout
Butter
Salt and pepper to taste
Corn husk, silk and ear removed

Clean trout and put knob of butter into stomach cavity. Season with salt and pepper. Wrap fish in corn husk. Close husk carefully around fish and tie closed with a piece of wire. Put husks around edge of campfire and cover with glowing coals for 15 minutes.

PLANKED TROUT

Fresh, whole trout
Butter

Clean, wash, and split trout. With skin side down, pin fish to a hardwood board and rub with butter. Hold over campfire, basting occasionally with more butter until done.

The two dishes are easy to make in the woods and are delicious. The use of corn husks is an old Indian method.

STUFFED TROUT

1 medium onion
5 Tbsp butter
1 cup breadcrumbs
1/2 tsp sage
Salt and pepper
2 medium trout (about 1 lb)
1/2 cup white wine

Chop onion and fry lightly in 3 Tbsp of the butter. Add breadcrumbs and seasoning. Clean trout and stuff with mixture. Place in greased baking dish and bake 10 minutes in 400°F oven. Baste with remaining butter, add wine, and cook another 10 minutes, basting often.

Fishing party

SOUSED MACKEREL OR HERRING

6 mackerel or herring
2 onions
1/2 cup water
1 cup white vinegar
1 tsp salt
1 tsp sugar
2 Tbsp pickling spice

Clean fish and remove bone, head, fins, and tail. Roll up fish individually and secure with a toothpick. Slice onions thinly and lay over and between fish. Place in a covered dish. Mix water, vinegar, salt, sugar, and spices and pour over fish. Bake in 350°F oven 1 1/2 hours.

STUFFED MACKEREL OR HERRING

2 mackerel or herring, split
1 Tbsp drippings
2 Tbsp oatmeal
1 tsp chopped parsley
Salt and pepper
Butter

Place one mackerel skin side down in greased baking dish. Mix drippings, oatmeal, and parsley. Spread on top of fish and cover with other fish, skin side up. Season and pat with knobs of butter. Bake in 350°F oven 30 minutes.

Herring entered the bays and waters around the island at the end of winter, just as the ice was melting. They made a plentiful and welcome change from salted meat and fish, and gave pioneers an opportunity to restock a depleted larder. Later in the year, islanders caught herring in large numbers and restocked in preparation for another winter. Dried, smoked, salted, or soused, they were a staple food.

A scavenger, mackerel is not often considered good eating. But if fresh, it is delicious—and nourishing. Now caught in nets, it was fished by line and hook in the last century.

Furnishing company, Montague, c. 1900

MOULES A LA MARINIERE

4 shallots
2 sprigs parsley
3 Tbsp butter
1 cup dry white wine
2 sprigs thyme
1 bay leaf
Freshly ground black pepper
5 dozen mussels
1 Tbsp flour

Finely chop shallots and parsley and sauté in 1 Tbsp butter. Add wine, thyme, bay leaf, and pepper and simmer gently 10 minutes. Add mussels, cover, and steam until shells open. Take mussels out and put in deep serving dish, removing top shells. Make a thickened sauce from half of remaining liquid, flour, and remaining butter. Pour over mussels before serving.

RAYMOND'S MUSSELS

2 dozen fresh mussels
2 onions
1 clove garlic
2 Tbsp lemon juice

Wash mussels carefully to remove any sand or grit and discard any that are not tightly closed. Finely chop onions and crush garlic. Place in heated pan and add lemon juice. Add mussels and cover. Cook approximately 3 to 5 minutes until mussels open. Serve immediately.

Note: It is best to use mussels as soon as possible after they have been collected, but, if necessary, they can be stored 2 to 3 days in a cool, damp place or in the refrigerator.

Wigwam, Rocky Point

STEWED EEL

2 eels
Pinch mace
Salt and pepper
Sprig parsley, chopped
2 Tbsp butter
1 cup stock

Skin and clean eels and cut into 2-inch lengths. Place in greased baking dish and sprinkle with mace, salt, pepper, and parsley. Dot with a little butter. Add stock, cover, and bake in 375°F oven 1 1/2 hours.

Skinning eels quickly and efficiently was one of the accomplishments of a pioneer wife. This was done most easily using a nail driven into a window frame or some other convenient spot. The eel should have its neck slit just below the head, leaving the backbone uncut. A string is then tied round the flesh and attached to the nail. The skin can be peeled off with a pair of pliers. Before cooking, the eel must be gutted. It helps to cut a slit lengthwise along the backbone to stop the eel from jumping around in the pan.

Shipbuilding, 1902

WINE-BAKED SMELTS

1 lb smelts
2 medium onions
2 stalks celery
1 cup dry white wine
Salt and pepper
2 Tbsp melted butter
Grated cheese

Clean, wash, and dry smelts. Chop onions and celery and place in greased baking dish. Lay smelts on top and add wine. Season and brush with butter. Bake in 375°F oven 15 minutes. Remove and sprinkle with cheese. Place under grill and cook until cheese is melted.

These small, silvery fish were favourites with early settlers. They enter island rivers in early spring when the ice is still solid and can be taken with bait and spears, or in nets set below the ice.

Simpson's Mill, Cavendish, 1898

SOLE AND MUSSELS

1 or 2 sole (enough for 4 fillets)
1 medium carrot, chopped
1 medium onion, chopped
Salt and pepper
1 tsp lemon juice
Butter
24 mussels
1 cup white sauce
Sprig parsley, chopped

Bone and skin sole to give 4 fillets. Place bones, skin, carrot, onion, salt, and pepper in a pot to make stock. Simmer gently about 30 minutes. Put fillets in baking dish, season, and sprinkle with lemon juice. Dot with butter and bake in 375°F oven approximately 10 minutes. Pour stock off and set aside, substituting for milk in favourite white sauce recipe. Cook mussels (see Raymond's Mussels) and stir into sauce. Pour over sole and garnish.

This is a very old recipe.

Construction of the Victoria chimes, 1918

ALMOND POTATOES

1/2 lb cooked potatoes
2 oz grated cheese
1/2 oz butter, melted
Salt and pepper
1 egg yolk
1 egg, beaten
1/2 cup crushed, blanched almonds

Mash potatoes and mix in cheese. Add butter, seasoning, and egg yolk, mixing well. Form into balls and coat with egg. Roll in crushed almonds to cover and fry in hot fat until brown.

POTATO PUFFS

3 cups cooked potatoes
2 eggs
Large knob of butter
Milk

Mash potatoes. Separate eggs and beat yolks into potatoes with butter and a little milk. Beat whites and fold in. Place in oven-proof casserole and bake in 375°F oven until nicely browned.

Note: This may be used as a topping for pies or by itself as a vegetable dish.

Gt. George and Richmond from Province House, Charlottetown, 1894

CHEESE POTATOES

1 lb boiled potatoes
1 oz butter
1 cup milk
Salt and pepper
2 oz grated cheese

Mash potatoes to a smooth mixture and add butter, milk, and seasoning, making sure to mix well. Mix two-thirds of cheese into potato mixture, sprinkle rest on top, and brown under grill.

POTATO-CHEESE HOTPOT

8 medium potatoes
1/3 cup butter
1/3 cup milk
Salt and pepper
2 eggs
1 cup grated Cheddar cheese
1/4 cup grated Parmesan cheese
1/2 cup breadcrumbs
1/4 cup sliced almonds

Boil potatoes until tender, then mash with butter and milk. Season to taste. Beat eggs gently and stir into potatoes with both cheeses. Put mixture into greased baking dish. Saute breadcrumbs and almonds in a little additional butter; spread over top. Bake uncovered in 350°F oven 20 minutes.

Horse and buggy on country road

POTATO CROQUETTES

1/2 lb cooked potatoes
1 oz butter, melted
Salt and pepper
1 egg
1 cup breadcrumbs

Mash potatoes and add butter, seasoning, and yolk of egg. Shape potato mixture into croquettes or balls, coat with egg white, and roll in breadcrumbs. Fry in hot fat until brown.

NEW POTATOES

New potatoes
Melted butter
Oatmeal, parsley, basil, or chives
Salt and pepper

Wash and, if necessary, scrub potatoes until clean, but do not peel. Boil until tender and drain. Roll in melted butter and in oatmeal or in one of the herbs. Season and serve hot with butter.

Note: Fresh, new potatoes are delicious after eating old potatoes through the winter. They are best cooked simply, but be careful not to overcook. Cold leftovers go well with a milk pudding.

POTATO CHIPS

Potatoes
Cooking oil

Peel potatoes and slice very thinly. A potato slicer can be used for small potatoes. Soak slices 1 hour in cold water and dry thoroughly in a cloth. Fry in hot fat until nicely browned. Drain and serve.

Montague Drugstore

FIDDLEHEADS

1 lb fiddleheads
1 small onion
1 tsp salt and pepper
2 cups water
Juice of 1 lemon
1/2 cup olive oil

Clean fiddleheads carefully. Finely chop onion and place in pan with all ingredients except fiddleheads. Bring to a boil and add fiddleheads. Cover and simmer gently 10 to 15 minutes. Remove, drain, and allow to cool. Chill before serving.

BEAN SALAD

Salad:
2 cups raw kidney beans
1 cup green beans
1 cup yellow beans
1 cup mushrooms
1/2 cup green pepper
1/4 cup onion
2 Tbsp fresh parsley
Dressing:
1 clove garlic
1/2 cup malt vinegar
1/4 cup olive oil
1/4 cup white wine
1 1/2 tsp liquid honey
1/2 tsp oregano
2 tsp Worcestershire sauce

To make dressing, crush garlic and mix with all wet ingredients and spices. Leave overnight to marinate.

Cook kidney beans and lightly cook other beans. Cut green and yellow beans into 1-inch lengths, slice mushrooms and pepper, chop onion, and finely chop parsley. Place in bowl and pour dressing over. Stir gently to mix. Chill before serving.

Mowing hay on a farm near Peakes Road and Bangor Road

DATE AND OATMEAL CAKE WITH LEMON-BUTTER ICING

Cake:

3/4 cup water

1 cup rolled oats

1 1/2 cups chopped dates

1 cup brown sugar

1 cup white sugar

1 cup butter or margarine

3 eggs, beaten

2 cups flour

1 tsp baking soda

2 tsp baking powder

1 tsp cinnamon

1 tsp salt

Icing:

1/4 cup butter

2 cups icing sugar

1/4 tsp lemon rind

2 tsp lemon juice

Boil water and mix with oats and dates in bowl. Let stand 20 minutes. Rub all sugar into butter and combine with eggs, adding a little of the flour as necessary to prevent curdling. Sift all dry ingredients and mix everything together. Pour into greased 12-inch-by-9-inch pan and bake in 350°F oven 45 minutes or until done.

Prepare icing. Mix all ingredients together and beat until creamy.

St. Paul's Rectory (now Richmond Centre Clinic), c. 1900

SULTANA CAKE

1 cup butter
2 cups sugar
3 eggs
3 1/2 cups flour
1 tsp baking powder
1 tsp baking soda
1/4 tsp salt
1 lb sultanas
1/4 lb red cherries
1/4 lb green cherries
1 cup milk
1 tsp lemon juice
1 tsp vanilla extract

Cream together butter and sugar. Add eggs alternately with a little of the flour to stop curdling and mix well. Sift together other dry ingredients. Add fruit to flour and mix to prevent sticking. Add dry ingredients to creamed mixture alternately with milk and mix well. Stir in lemon juice and vanilla. Pour into loaf pan and bake 1 1/2 hours in 300°F oven.

Souris Station, c. 1895

CARROT CAKE

Cake:
1 medium orange
3 1/2 cups grated carrot
1 cup walnuts
1 cup raisins
1 cup vegetable oil
1 1/2 cups brown sugar
4 eggs
1 tsp vanilla
1 cup whole-wheat flour
1 cup all-purpose flour
1 1/2 tsp baking powder
1 1/2 tsp baking soda
1 tsp nutmeg
1 tsp allspice
1 tsp cinnamon
1 tsp salt
Glaze:
Grated peel and juice of 1 large orange
3/4 cup sugar

Grate orange and add to carrots with walnuts and raisins. Add oil, sugar, eggs, and vanilla and mix well. Stir in dry ingredients and pour mixture into cake tin. Bake in 325°F oven 45 minutes or until cake is done.

Prepare glaze. Mix together orange peel, juice, and sugar. Add to cake while hot.

Faculty from Prince of Wales College, 1900

APPLESAUCE CAKE

2 cups flour
1 tsp baking soda
1/2 tsp cloves
1/2 tsp cinnamon
3/4 tsp salt
1/2 cup butter
1 cup brown sugar
1 egg
3 tsp vinegar
1 cup applesauce
2 tsp grated lemon rind
1 cup raisins

Sift together all dry ingredients except fruit and sugar. Cream butter and sugar. Add egg and beat, adding a little of the flour as necessary to avoid curdling. Combine all ingredients and mix well. Pour into 8-inch-square pan and bake 45 minutes in 350°F oven.

SPICY FRUIT CAKE

2 cups water
3/4 cup seedless raisins
1 cup white sugar
1/3 cup butter
1/2 tsp cinnamon
1/2 tsp nutmeg
1 egg
1 tsp salt

2 tsp baking soda
1/2 lb mixed peel
2 cups flour
1/2 cup chopped walnuts

Bring water to a boil and add raisins, sugar, butter, and spices. Boil 10 minutes and allow to cool. Beat egg and add with all other ingredients, mixing well. Bake in loaf pan in 325°F oven 1 1/2 to 2 hours.

Railway officials at Senator Robertson's house, Montague, 1906

OLD-FASHIONED CHOCOLATE CAKE

1/2 cup butter
1 1/4 cups white sugar
1/2 tsp salt
1 tsp vanilla extract
2 eggs
6 Tbsp melted unsweetened chocolate
1 3/4 cups flour
1 tsp baking soda
1 cup sour milk

Cut butter and sugar together and add salt, vanilla, and eggs. Add melted chocolate and beat well. Sift flour and soda together and add alternately with milk. Pour mixture into greased pan and bake in 350°F oven 30 to 40 minutes.

Note: If sour milk is not available, use fresh milk mixed with 1 Tbsp vinegar.

The Legislative Assembly, 1908

PUMPKIN PIE

3 eggs
1 cup cooked pumpkin
3/4 cup brown sugar
1 cup milk
1/2 tsp nutmeg
1/2 tsp ginger
3 drops maple syrup
1/2 tsp salt
Pastry for pie

Beat eggs. Mix all ingredients together and beat well. Pour into pie shell, brush with a little milk, and bake in 350°F oven about 1 hour. Filling should be firm and crust should be golden brown.

APPLE PIE

3 Tbsp flour
1 cup sugar
4 cups sliced apples
Pastry for pie
1 Tbsp butter
Large pinch cinnamon
Milk

Mix flour and sugar in bowl and roll apples in mixture to cover. Place in pastry-lined pie dish, dot with butter, and sprinkle on cinnamon. Cover with top crust and brush with milk. Bake in 400°F oven 30 minutes or until pastry is done.

Advertising a minstrel show in front of Dodd & Rogers Hardware Co., c. 1900

STRAWBERRY DESSERT

1 cup flour
1/4 cup brown sugar
1/2 cup chopped walnuts
1/2 cup melted butter
1 cup white sugar
2 egg whites
2 Tbsp lemon juice
2 1/2 cups sliced strawberries
1 cup whipped cream

Mix flour, brown sugar, walnuts, and melted butter. Put mixture into baking pan and bake in 350°F oven 20 minutes, stirring occasionally to make crumbs. Remove dried crumbs from pan and use two-thirds to make dessert base in another baking dish. Combine sugar, egg whites, lemon juice, and strawberries in large bowl and beat until mixture can form stiff peaks. Fold in whipped cream and pour over base. Sprinkle top with remaining crumbs and freeze overnight. Before serving, garnish with fresh strawberries and cream.

Women spinning

BLUEBERRY DELIGHT

2 cups flour
1/2 tsp salt
2 1/2 tsp baking powder
1 cup sugar
1/2 cup butter
1/2 cup milk
2 cups blueberries
1/2 tsp cinnamon
1/2 cup melted butter

Mix flour, salt, baking powder, and 1 1/2 Tbsp of the sugar together and rub in 1/2 cup butter. Add milk to make a dough and roll out to about 1/2 inch thick. Square off and fit into greased pan. Place blueberries in middle, folding each corner towards centre to cover blueberries but leave a space about 4 inches across. Bake in 400°F oven 20 minutes or until dough begins to brown. Remove from oven and switch oven off. Make topping by mixing cinnamon, melted butter, and remaining sugar. Poke into folded area to mix with blueberries and return to cooling oven. Leave 15 minutes. Serve hot, garnished with whipped cream and additional blueberries.

Kindergarten children planting trees, Arbour Day, 1898

BREAD-AND-BUTTER PUDDING

4 slices bread
Butter
1 cup milk
1/4 cup sugar
2 eggs, beaten
Pinch nutmeg

Butter bread and cut into bite-sized pieces. Put into baking bowl and cover with mixture of milk, sugar, and beaten egg. Bake in 350°F oven 30 minutes. Sprinkle nutmeg on top and serve immediately.

Note: If desired, raisins or chopped dates can be added before cooking.

PLUM PUDDING

2 apples
Juice and grated rind 1 lemon
1/4 lb flour
1/4 lb breadcrumbs
1/2 lb sugar
3/4 lb currants
3/4 lb raisins
1/4 lb mixed peel
1 heaping tsp salt
1/4 tsp cinnamon
1/4 tsp cloves
1/4 tsp nutmeg

6 eggs
1/2 cup molasses
1/2 cup brandy
1 lb suet

Peel, core, and dice apples. Mix together dry ingredients and sift in spices. Beat eggs gently and mix everything together, adding a little milk if necessary. Boil in greased pudding bowl 3 to 4 hours, or 1 1/2 hours in pressure cooker.

SS Stanley *and crew, pre-1900*

SCOTS SHORTBREAD

8 oz flour
2 oz sugar
4 oz butter

Mix flour and sugar. Cut in, then rub in, butter. Knead well and press mixture into pan so it is about 1/2 to 3/4 of an inch thick. Prick top with fork for decoration and bake in 325°F oven 30 minutes or until shortbread begins to turn golden brown. Remove from oven and allow to cool a few minutes. Cut into slices and allow to cool further before removing from pan.

OATCAKES

Pinch baking soda
2 tsp salt
1 lb oatmeal
1 oz drippings, melted
Hot water

Add soda and salt to oatmeal and pour in drippings. Add enough hot water to make a soft mixture. Divide into two parts and knead well, working mixture on wooden board. Roll out thinly and cut into circles with cup or glass. Rub with dry oatmeal to whiten and cook on hot, ungreased pan. Cook a few minutes on one side and turn, or cook other side under grill.

Ready to board?

POTATO CANDY

4 cups icing sugar
4 cups unsweetened, shredded coconut
3/4 cup cold, mashed potato
1/2 tsp salt
1 1/2 tsp vanilla extract
1/2 lb sweet chocolate

Mix icing sugar and coconut into potato. Add salt and vanilla and mix well. Press mixture firmly into large pan. Melt chocolate and pour over. Cut when cool.

VANILLA FUDGE

1 lb sugar
2 oz butter
1 cup milk
1 Tbsp corn syrup
1 tsp vanilla extract

Put sugar, butter, milk, and syrup in pan and bring slowly to a boil, stirring occasionally. Stir continuously while boiling and test occasionally by dropping a little mixture into cold water. It is ready when drop can be picked up after a few minutes and rolled into a soft ball. At that point, remove from heat. Add vanilla and beat until mixture begins to show a grain. Pour into greased pan and cut when cool.

Charlottetown Water Works, c. 1899

HOT CROSS BUNS

2 Tbsp butter
1/4 cup sugar
1/2 tsp salt
1 cup scalded milk
1 pkg baker's yeast
1/2 tsp cinnamon
1/4 tsp cloves
1 cup rye or whole-wheat flour
2 cups white flour

1/4 cup raisins
1/4 cup currants
1 egg, well beaten

Mix butter, sugar, and salt. Add scalded milk and, when cooled to lukewarm, add yeast. Sift spices and flour and add. Add fruit and egg. Knead on floured board, cover, and allow to rise until doubled in size. Shape buns in well-greased pan, allowing space between for rising. Cut a cross on top of each bun with sharp, greased knife. Let buns rise again and bake in 400°F oven 15 to 20 minutes.

GINGERBREAD

1/2 cup sugar
1/2 cup butter and lard mixed
1 cup molasses
1 egg, beaten
2 1/2 cups flour
1/2 tsp salt
1 tsp cinnamon
1/2 tsp cloves
1 tsp ginger
1 1/2 tsp baking soda
1 cup water

Cream sugar and shortening. Add molasses and egg with a little of the flour to stop curdling. Sift dry ingredients together and add to shortening. Heat water but do not boil, and add last. Beat until smooth and put in greased baking dish. Bake in 350°F oven 40 minutes or until done.

Note: This is a very old recipe. All butter can be used instead of the mixture of lard and butter.

Souris Methodist Church Picnic, Grant's Crossing, 1917

CRANBERRY-NUT BREAD

2 cups flour
1 cup sugar
1 tsp salt
1 1/2 tsp baking powder
1/2 tsp baking soda
1/4 cup butter
1 egg
3/4 cup orange juice
1 Tbsp grated orange rind
1/2 cup chopped walnuts
2 cups fresh cranberries

Sift dry ingredients together and rub in butter. Beat egg and mix with orange juice and rind. Pour onto flour and stir in, but do not beat or overstir. Fold in nuts and cranberries. Put in greased baking tin and bake in 350°F oven about 1 hour or until ready. Cut when cool.

APPLE-NUT BREAD

1/2 cup butter
2/3 cup sugar
2 eggs
2 cups flour
1 tsp baking powder
1/2 tsp salt
1 tsp baking soda
1/4 cup chopped walnuts
1 cup grated apple

Rub butter and sugar together. Beat eggs and add with a little of the flour to stop mixture from curdling. Sift dry ingredients together and stir in. Add walnuts and apple and mix well. Pour mixture into greased baking pan and bake in 350°F oven about 1 hour or until ready. Do not cut until cool and firm.

Tea at Government House with Dr. A.C. MacDonald, c. 1918

SODA BREAD

1 cup all-purpose flour
2 cups whole-wheat flour
1/2 tsp salt
1 tsp baking soda
2 tsp sugar
4 oz margarine
1 1/4 cups buttermilk

Sift dry ingredients together. Add margarine and blend with fingers. Add milk and knead well. Shape into an oval loaf and place on greased pan. Bake 30 minutes in 400°F oven. Reduce heat to 350°F and bake another 30 minutes.

BAKING-POWDER BISCUITS

2 cups flour
4 tsp baking powder
1 tsp salt
2 Tbsp sugar
4 Tbsp butter
1 egg
Milk

Mix dry ingredients and sift well. Blend in butter with fingers. Beat egg slightly and add milk to make 1 cup. Stir into mixture. Roll out gently and cut into shapes. Bake in 400°F oven about 10 minutes or until brown.

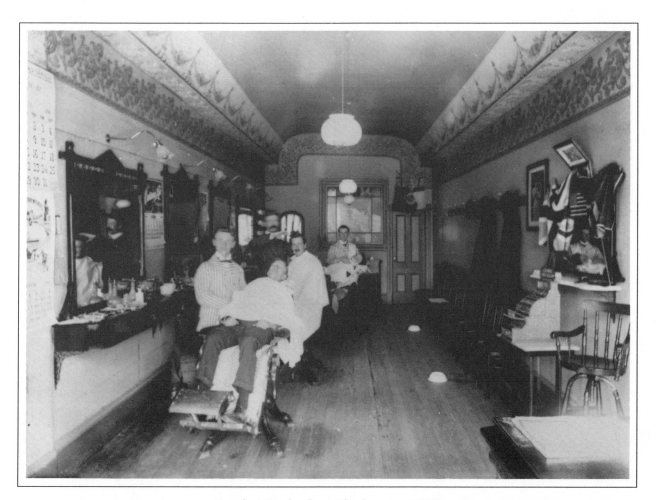

Rearden's Barbershop, Charlottetown, 1899

CRANBERRY MUFFINS

3 cups fresh cranberries
1/2 cup icing sugar
2 cups flour
1/2 cup sugar
1/2 tsp salt
3 tsp baking powder
1 egg
1 cup milk
4 Tbsp melted butter

Cut cranberries in half and coat with icing sugar. Mix dry ingredients together. Beat egg and add with milk and butter to flour mixture. Mix well and fold in cranberries. Put into muffin tins or papers and bake 20 minutes in 350°F oven.

BLUEBERRY MUFFINS

2 cups flour
3 tsp baking powder
1/2 cup sugar
1 tsp salt
2 eggs
3/4 cup milk
4 Tbsp melted butter
1 cup blueberries

Mix dry ingredients together. Beat eggs and mix with milk and butter. Stir milk mixture into dry ingredients and gently fold in blueberries, taking care not to break them. Spoon into greased muffin tins and bake in 400°F oven 15 minutes.

Berries were great favourites of pioneer children, who could eat and enjoy themselves while helping with the chore of collecting food for the family.

McDonald Consolidated School, 1910

CRANBERRY JELLY

4 cups cranberries
2 cups water
2 cups sugar

Boil cranberries in water until soft and strain through a jelly bag. Add sugar and heat until boiling. Boil until thick (about 10 minutes) stirring continuously. Pour into heated, sterilized jelly jars.

STRAWBERRY JAM

4 lb strawberries in good condition
4 lb sugar

Clean strawberries and allow to dry. Heat in large pan until juice begins to flow (about 15 minutes). Add sugar and boil rapidly 15 minutes. Skim and allow to cool 5 to 10 minutes. Stir and pour into clean, heated jam jars.

BLACKCURRANT JAM

3 lb blackcurrants
3 pts water
6 lb sugar

Wash fruit, put in a pan with water, and bring to a boil. Simmer about 10 minutes until skins are soft. Add sugar and stir until it is dissolved. Boil quickly about 20 minutes or until jam reaches setting point. Test by pouring a small amount onto a cool saucer. Allow to cool a few minutes and bottle.

Masons' meeting, c. 1900

GREEN-TOMATO CHUTNEY

4 lb green tomatoes
1 lb apples
1 lb shallots
1/2 lb seedless raisins
1/2 oz whole ginger
12 chillies
1 lb brown sugar
1 pt vinegar
1/2 oz salt
1 Tbsp molasses
4 tsp cornstarch

Cut up tomatoes, peel, core, and cut up apples, chop shallots and raisins. Crush ginger and chillies and tie up in a small, muslin bag. Put all ingredients in pan, bring to a boil, and simmer until soft. Add cornstarch to thicken. Remove spice bag and bottle chutney.

RHUBARB CHUTNEY

2 lb rhubarb
1 lb onions
1 1/2 lb sugar
1 lb sultanas
1 oz salt
1 oz ginger
1 tsp black pepper
1 tsp cloves
1 pt malt vinegar

Wash rhubarb and cut into small pieces. Skin and slice onions. Place rhubarb and onion in large pan and add remaining ingredients. Boil slowly 45 minutes or until thick. Put into warm jars and seal.

Woodworking shed

MAYONNAISE

2 cups water
4 eggs
4 Tbsp flour
1 cup vinegar
1 Tbsp salt
1/2 cup sugar
1 Tbsp mustard
1/2 tsp pepper

Boil water, beat eggs, and mix all ingredients together. Place in double boiler and cook until thick, stirring occasionally at first and more often as mixture begins to thicken.

PICKLED BEETS

12 lb small beets
3 sticks cinnamon
1 Tbsp pickling spice
1 Tbsp whole cloves
6 cups brown sugar
6 cups vinegar

Boil beets until tender and peel when cool enough. While beets are boiling, make a spice bag of cinnamon, pickling spice, and cloves secured in a piece of muslin. Tie tightly and boil 15 minutes in a mixture of the sugar and vinegar. Remove and discard spice bag. Place beets in sterilized jars and pour liquid over them before sealing jars tightly.

R. Small's Tin Shop, Charlottetown, c. 1900

GOOSEBERRY WINE

8 lb gooseberries
2 gallons water
3 lb sugar to each gallon juice

Wash berries and cut ends off. Crush fruit well and put in wooden tub or large earthenware crock. Add water and mix well. Cover and leave 2 days. Strain off liquid and add correct amount of sugar, stirring until all sugar is dissolved. Put into a cask and let stand in warm place until fermentation has ceased. Drive a cork in securely. Fit a peg into cork and pull it out every 1 or 2 days to allow any gas to escape. When all action has ceased, close tightly and leave 9 months in a cool place. Bottle.

Note: Collect gooseberries before they change colour in the fall.

BLACKCURRANT CORDIAL

6 lb blackcurrants
6 lb sugar

Mix together fruit and sugar. Put into a stone jar, cover, and leave 8 weeks, stirring once or twice a week. Strain off liquid and pour into clean bottles, corking loosely until fermentation has ceased. Cork tightly.

Note: To make an excellent summer drink from the mash strained off the juice, add approximately 1 gallon cold water and shake well. Strain and bottle.

These old recipes relied on the presence of wild yeasts. It would be advisable today to use a more modern recipe, along with a good wine yeast and proper fermentation locks.

Charlottetown Golf Club, c. 1880